DATING WHILE AUTISTIC

Cut Through the Social Quagmire
and Find Your Person

Part 2 of the Book Series *Adulting while Autistic*

Wendela Whitcomb Marsh, MA, RSD

DATING WHILE AUTISTIC
Cut Through the Social Quagmire and Find Your Person

All marketing and publishing rights guaranteed to and reserved by:

FUTURE HORIZONS

(817) 277-0727

(817) 277-2270 (fax)

E-mail: info@fhautism.com

www.fhautism.com

ISBN: 9781949177992

This book is written in memory
of the author of my love story,
David Scott Marsh

and for our own
Cat David Robinson Marsh
Siobhan Eleanor Wise Marsh
Noel Maebh Whitcomb Marsh

Contents

Introduction to DATING WHILE AUTISTIC vii

Chapter 1: Manage Expectations 1
    Not Everyone You Like Will Like You

Chapter 2: Flirty or Friendly 11
    How Can You Tell?

Chapter 3: How to Chat 23
    Let's Talk About That

Chapter 4: Respect Boundaries 37
    Don't Overstep, and Don't Get Stepped Over

Chapter 5: Sense & Sensory Sensibility 53
    It's Different for Everyone

Chapter 6: Interests 67
    Yours, Mine, and Ours

Chapter 7: Speed Limits 79
    The Slower Partner Sets the Pace

Chapter 8: Happy Endings Happen 95
    In Their Own Sweet Time

Acknowledgments 109

Introduction to

DATING WHILE AUTISTIC

"There are two basic motivating forces: fear and love. When we are afraid, we pull back from life. When we are in love, we open to all that life has to offer with passion, excitement, and acceptance."

— John Lennon, singer-songwriter

"We're all a little weird. And life is a little weird. And when we find someone whose weirdness is compatible with ours, we join up with them and fall into mutually satisfying weirdness—and call it love—true love."

— Robert Fulghum, author of *True Love*

Introduction

We've all heard the happily-ever-after fairy tales. People love to fall in love, but it's not always smooth sailing. For some autistic people, especially those who struggle with social communication and emotional regulation, it can seem impossibly out of reach.

But why shouldn't that ideal love match be possible for everyone?

I know that this dream is attainable. I was married for almost twenty-seven years to a wonderful man who was a devoted husband and father, and who was also autistic. We didn't know he was autistic when we fell in love and married, but I knew and loved the person he was.

If you're reading this book, you may wonder if you'll ever find true love for yourself. No one can see the future or promise a fairy tale outcome, but I can say with confidence that the possibilities are wide open. A loving relationship should never be ruled out just because of a diagnosis.

Does that mean the way will be smooth and that you can have whatever person you fancy as your true love? No, of course not. But this isn't promised to neuromajority people, either. It's important to be open to what the future may hold for you, even if it's not exactly what you first had in mind. Most worthwhile things require work, and love is no different.

Dating While Autistic

To help you move forward with this work, this book takes a close look at dating and romance and provides strategies and tips to help you move from a first date to friendship to love.

You may notice that I often use identity-first language here, saying "autistic person" rather than "person with autism." That's because most of the autistic people I know have told me they prefer identity-first language. Sometimes you may see me use person-first language, with phrases like "on the spectrum." This is because a few people have shared that they prefer person-first. I want to honor everyone's preference in some way, whether they are in the minority or majority. Every voice deserves to be heard.

Here are some more things you'll find in this book:

Bad Idea/Better Idea offers tips for what to avoid and what else you can try instead.

A Couple of Singles follows two fictional characters, Bill and Trish, who are each seeking a long-term romantic partner. Their stories will demonstrate the path to love with its many twists and turns, and illustrate how various ideas play out for them and how to recognize and avoid pitfalls they meet along their way.

Introduction

Ask Yourself provides questions for self-reflection. These may help you prioritize your values and focus on what's most important for you as you follow your heart in search of a romantic connection.

Actually Autistic Love Stories bring firsthand knowledge from neurodivergent couples who are already living the dream.

If you want down-to-earth guidance on how to navigate dating and relationships, you've come to the right place.

Here we go!

BAD IDEA/BETTER IDEA

You want to fall in love and have that perfect person who will be your life partner.

✗ **BAD IDEA:** However much you want this, you don't think you should have to go out of your way to look for that person. You just know that there is someone special out there for you, your soulmate, and you are destined to be together. Somehow, they will find you, you'll meet in some cute way, and you'll both know it's love. There's nothing for you to do but to sit back and wait for Cupid to shoot that arrow so that everything will fall into place for you.

✓ **BETTER IDEA:** You realize that just sitting around and waiting for that special someone to find you in your living room is not the answer. You decide to let your friends and family know that you are interested in meeting someone, in case they know somebody they can introduce you to. You find a safe dating app and set up your profile. You participate in singles gatherings in your faith community, local meet-up groups, and especially groups of people who are interested in the same things you are interested in. You find that you enjoy going to places where you might meet someone who shares your interests, and you make some new friends without setting unrealistic expectations of what might come of the friendships.

A COUPLE OF SINGLES

Bill

Bill is thirty-one years old. He lives with his parents and works from home for a tech company. He was diagnosed at age twelve with

Introduction

what they called Asperger's syndrome at the time and now under-stands that he is actually autistic. He would like to meet someone, fall in love, and get married someday. Now that he is in his thirties, he feels that he ought to move out of his parents' home. He could afford his own place, but he hesitates to look for an apartment on his own. He'd rather start his new life as a married man with a loving, supportive wife, happily choosing their own first home together. The problem is he doesn't know how to meet someone.

Trish

Trish is thirty-two years old. She works as an administrative assistant in the admissions office of the college she graduated from ten years ago. It's a "behind-the-scenes" job where she can hide behind her computer and avoid interacting with the public. She was diagnosed with what they called "high-functioning autism" when she was in school, but she does not identify with the functioning label. She has days when things go wrong and she is overwhelmed by sensory and social stress and can lose her ability to speak. That feels pretty "low-functioning" to her. However, she appears to function very well on a good day, and no one knows the cost of putting on her "high-functioning" mask. Trish would love to fall in love and have a life partner, but when her co-workers invite her to go to bars or clubs with them after work, she turns them down. She is so uncomfortable in those settings that even if she met someone, she probably wouldn't have the mental or emotional strength to engage in conversation with them. She wonders what she can do to find her match.

ASK YOURSELF

Before you even embark on this journey, ask yourself why. Why are you here, reading this book now? Maybe a family member or friend gave you the book because they think you should find someone. That's nice of them. But is it what you want? Many people imagine everyone would be happier going through life Noah's ark-style, two by two, because that is what they like. But not everyone has the same wish. If you're the recipient of a well-meaning but unwanted gift of this book, I hope you'll read it anyway. I worked hard on it, and I like it. But I want you to know: you should feel free to ignore it. If you don't want to be a couple, if you love your single life as it is, then forget all this. You be you. Don't let anyone else try to mold you into a neuromajority cookie cutter or expect you to mask who you are.

On the other hand, if you are single and looking for a life partner, you've come to the right place. I hope this book gives you new ideas to consider, confidence to step up, potential pitfalls to avoid, and optimism that you can have the relationship you want.

Introduction

So, ask yourself: Do you want a relationship?

ACTUALLY AUTISTIC LOVE STORIES

Kelsey's Story:

A couple of years after moving to a new city, I realized I was lonely and wanted to meet new people. I had friends from back home but no one to spend time with locally. I tried volunteering and met a few nice people, but no one that I actually wanted to befriend or date. After some thought, I realized that I actively avoided doing much in public spaces and that it would be very unlikely that I would meet people if that continued. (I do not have any social media accounts and knew that online dating was not for me.) Since I knew social media and online dating was not for me, and I wasn't ready to "put myself out there," I decided to tweak what I was already doing. One day, I decided to stay in the shared laundry room while I did my laundry. Normally I would drop off my clothes and head back to my apartment to do some chores, but this time I stayed put and read a book, thinking other people were likely stop in to do their laundry as well. If they wanted to talk, they would, and if they didn't, they would just do their laundry and leave. I was right!

Over the next several months, I met many different people, including some new friends and my now-husband, Doug. Doug and I met three times before he gave me his number, complete with a drawing of Pac-Man (the figure on his shirt that I recognized, which led me to initiate our third conversation.) There was also an invitation to go skunk watching. (I really love skunks, another thing that we discussed that day.) I texted him that day, we started spending time together, and the rest is history.

Doug's Story:

Kelsey and I had been living in the same apartment complex for a couple of years but had never met. We mostly kept to ourselves but occasionally had to use a communal laundry room.

After running into each other several times, we finally struck up a conversation while we did our laundry. Kelsey initiated the conversation by complimenting me on my video game T-shirt. The retro depiction of a mascot character (Pac-Man) reminded her of her father and brother. It was a quick social interaction about one of my passions. I could talk about video games all day, but I resisted.

Eventually the conversation turned to animals. I told Kelsey how I had reunited a group of ducklings with their mother. I showed her pictures and videos of the ducks. And she seemed to find this very endearing. We also talked about the resident skunks at our apartment complex and how they liked to root around in the pine needles.

Introduction

I finished folding my laundry and hastily left for my apartment, unsure of how to end the conversation. I wanted to ask Kelsey out, but I also didn't want to appear too forward or be rejected in person. I enjoyed talking with Kelsey, but if things ended poorly, I might never be able to go back to that particular laundry room again!

When I got back to my apartment, I quickly drew a picture of Pac-Man and wrote a note suggesting we go looking for skunks some time. I wrote down my number so she could text me. I thought texting was easier than talking on the phone, because we could think about what we wanted to say before we said it.

I ran back to the laundry room hoping to catch Kelsey before she left. I gave her the note and took off before I saw how she might react. If she didn't call or text, then I would know she wasn't interested. Fortunately, she texted me back, and we planned our first outing.

— Kelsey and Doug

Chapter 1

Manage Expectations

Not Everyone You Like Will Like You

"Never idealize others. They will never live up to your expectations. A growing relationship can only be nurtured by genuineness."

— Leo Buscaglia, author of *Love*

"I had these kind of unrealistic expectations that were fueled by romantic comedies, and it has both helped me and hurt me in many ways. It helped me because, in general, they've made me hopeful. I just figure things will eventually work out for me. But nobody is like any Tom Hanks character. Nobody is Hugh Grant. No one is Meg Ryan!"

— Mindy Kaling, American actress

Chapter 1: Manage Expectations

Unrealistic expectations about the way our life "should be" can keep us from ever being happy with the way our life actually is. We can't all fall in love with a famous, traditionally gorgeous movie star; there simply aren't enough of them to go around.

Fictional characters can't pick up the phone. But just because we can't all date the rich and beautiful few doesn't mean we need to lower our standards in the areas that really count.

Rather than judging potential dates on their outward appearance, look for someone who shares your values and your interests.

You might find someone who shares your values in a faith community, or a political party, or a nonprofit organization. Here you'll find people who believe in what you believe or who are working to make the world a better place in the same way you are. If you meet someone volunteering for a food bank, for instance, you will know that they care about feeding the hungry. If you go to the same church, then it's likely your religious values are in sync. Someone who volunteers at a no-kill animal shelter or fosters puppies or kittens to help them find their forever homes may be the one for you if you share a love of animals.

Examine your own values, and prioritize what is most important to you. What will continue to matter to you in five years, or ten, or fifty? Do you want a partner who votes and who leans politically in the same direction you do? Or someone with strong religious beliefs that are compatible with your own? Or a passion to speak up for those less fortunate or those who cannot speak for themselves? Getting clear on your own values will help you in your search for love.

What about shared interests? What would you like to do together? If you meet at a book club or hiking club, then it's probable that your potential date enjoys reading or the outdoors as much as you do. Passions or hobbies need not be shared completely but should at least be understood and appreciated. It's possible to have a happy, fulfilled relationship even if one of you loves Marvel and one DC, or one loves Tolkien and one *Game of Thrones*. My marriage is proof that even a match between a *Star Wars* fan and a Trekkie is not out of the question. It may be an unrealistic expectation that your partner should share everything you love to the same degree, but it is not unrealistic to expect that each of you will respect and value each other's special interests, or "spins."

BAD IDEA/BETTER IDEA

You have an ideal person in mind who will be your soul mate.

✗ **BAD IDEA:** One thing you're sure of is that the person for you will be drop-dead gorgeous. Why shouldn't a beautiful person

Chapter 1: Manage Expectations

want to date you, even if you're what some would consider "not in the same league?" There's nothing wrong with how you look, and they shouldn't be so shallow as to reject you based on your physical appearance. If they got to know you, they would see what a great person you are. It would be completely unfair of them to pass you up based on your looks alone. The problem is, you are also judging them on looks alone, wanting someone based on their physical beauty rather than who they are on the inside. This is a two-way street. If you don't want to be sized up based only on your appearance, don't look for a date based on theirs.

✓ **BETTER IDEA:** You dream of meeting "the one," but you have no idea what they will look like. You know that if you're going to spend the next fifty years as a couple, you will both lose your youthful appearance, and other, more substantial charms will be more important. You're looking for someone to share your values and interests. They might not look like the romantic leads you see in the movies, but that's okay. You'd rather have a lot in common and enjoy the same things. Chances are good that if you start off liking each other and, over time, grow to care for one another and fall in love, the way they look will become your new definition of gorgeous.

Dating While Autistic

A COUPLE OF SINGLES

Bill

Bill decided to try an online dating service. He was encouraged to see so many beautiful women on the site. As he started contacting them, though, he realized that many of them seemed to be overly focused on money. When they found out that he lived with his parents, many of them ghosted him.

One woman kept texting him and said it was fine with her that he lived with his parents. She wanted to fly to his city to meet him and his parents and build a future together. She seemed so sure that Bill was the right man for her, and she couldn't wait to be with him. The only problem was that she needed money for air fare. Bill almost wired her some money, but then he stopped to think about it. Did it make sense for a person to leave their home and job to move across the country to be with someone they've never even met? He wondered if she had good judgment. When he did not immediately offer to send her the money, her tone changed. She alternated between angry demands, childish whines, and sexy come-ons. Bill didn't even know who she was anymore. He asked to have a video meeting so they could talk about it face-to-face instead of just texting, but she always had an excuse. She finally agreed, but on the day of their video date, she said the camera on her phone didn't work.

Chapter 1: Manage Expectations

By now, Bill had decided that she was most likely a con artist trying to get his money with no real desire to meet him at all. It was hurtful, but it was a learning experience for him. He had high expectations that the beautiful pictures on the dating app all represented lovely people who, like him, were looking for true love, but this was not the reality. He had to adjust his expectations. Next time, he would not be so easily fooled.

Trish

Trish thought it would be a good idea to join a church to meet someone. Her parents had gone to the same church when they met, and they were happy, so it made sense. She looked online and found a church that had a young adults' social group. Trish showed up at the church on the day of the meeting and walked hesitantly into the social hall. She saw three couples and one lone man having coffee and cookies. The man made a beeline for her as soon as she walked in. He started asking her about herself and telling her all about himself, until she felt overwhelmed. It seemed that he had been the only single in the group for a long time, and when she walked in, he thought his prayers had been answered. She must be the one for him! Except, Trish didn't feel that way at all. She had hoped to sit on the sidelines of the group and just observe and see what it was like. This guy was putting her in the spotlight, and it made her extremely uncomfortable. Before long, she made an excuse and left early. She had expected that it would be easy to find someone to date in a church group and was dismayed by how the evening went. The dynamics of this particular group were such that she could not avoid being noticed and singled out. The experience put her off for a while but did not discourage her completely. She'd try to manage her expectations next time.

ASK YOURSELF

- What values are most important to you?
- Is it non-negotiable for you that your partner shares your faith?
- Your political leanings?
- Your interests?
- With this self-knowledge, where are you most likely to meet someone?
- Knowing what is most important to you will help you to not get bogged down in the small stuff, manage your own expectations, and put yourself in places where your ideal partner is most likely to be found.

Chapter 1: Manage Expectations

ACTUALLY AUTISTIC LOVE STORIES

Online dating was finally becoming less stigmatized, and I knew I needed to find someone who shared my progressive values. (It was January of 2017, and I had a lot of strong feelings about the person who had just been inaugurated.) So I made myself a Tinder account to get some vetting out of the way before expending too much social energy on dead-end dates. By some stroke of dumb luck, Zach also made a Tinder account to try and find some friends in our city.

We were both very honest about ourselves on our profiles, which is why I think we found each other. I was drawn in by his promises of a dinner date with mustard Rorschach napkin readings and his love of "pretentious music," as he put it.

We talked for a few weeks, our text exchanges becoming more frequent, before I got the courage to ask him on a date. I was becoming increasingly infatuated with "Art Rock Cutie," as I referred to him with my friends.

We agreed to meet at an artsy bar and restaurant downtown the day before Valentine's Day. It's my go-to first date spot—I knew the line cook and how to exit through the back if I just couldn't handle the exchange any longer. I had been buzzing in anticipation of the date the whole day.

Dating While Autistic

He was sweet, a little quiet, goofy, and charming. Apparently he spent the first part of the date thinking I was uninterested because I was so nervous (and frankly, I checked my phone a few times out of anxiety). After we had a drink and loosened up, the conversation started really flowing. We over-shared a bit and felt shockingly comfortable together.

—Julie and Zach

Chapter 2

Flirty or Friendly

How Can You Tell?

"I don't know what flirting is really. Sometimes, in women, friendliness comes across as flirting. That is not what it is."

— Rita Ora, British singer

"My version of flirting is looking at someone I find attractive and hoping they're braver than I am."

— Cheryl Payne

Chapter 2: Flirty or Friendly

Often people give advice about dating and flirting such as "Always be yourself." This seems obvious. Who else would you be? But perhaps this advice is meant to reassure you that you are perfectly fine just as you are, with no need to mask, put on a persona, or pretend to be cooler than you feel.

Other advice you may have heard: "Make eye contact, but don't stare." Now you may find yourself counting the seconds. How long do you look at their eyes? How often should you glance away, and when do you look back? For that matter, which eye are you supposed to be looking at? Will they notice if you look at their eyebrows instead of their eyes? There's just so much going on with eyes. It's important to listen to what the person you like is saying to you, even if you don't feel particularly comfortable with eye contact.

Some people have memorized clever pick-up lines from the internet, but beware. Many of these are actually disrespectful or body-focused, or they come on too strong. (If you say they have a beautiful body, for instance, they may be turned off and not receive it in the way you might have hoped.) It's hard for someone to get to know you if all they hear from you are internet come-ons. So, drop the memorized lines and speak your truth in the moment.

This might mean actually saying something like, "I'm the kind of person who can never tell if someone is trying to flirt with me or just being nice. I like you and I hope you like me, but I'm not going to assume anything unless you come right out and say so." Side note: Please don't memorize the preceding statement and recite it to someone you like. Find your own version, in your own voice, and say what is true for you. It should come from the heart, not from the page.

On the other hand, for those who like to script out possible conversations in advance, do whatever makes you comfortable. Just let the script be of your own feelings and not copied from someone else, unless that other person spoke your truth in a way that resonated with you.

The truth is lots of people are uncomfortable with flirting and wondering what the other person is thinking. If you come right out and say how you feel, it may be refreshing. If they like you, they will be glad to know that you like them even if flirting isn't your preferred language. If they don't like you in that way, better to find out sooner rather than spending a lot of time wondering.

Knowing the truth about how someone feels about you can free you up to find someone better suited for you.

BAD IDEA/BETTER IDEA

You see someone at a social gathering, and you find yourself immediately drawn to them. They seem so attractive and fun, you'd love to get to know them better.

Chapter 2: Flirty or Friendly

✗ **BAD IDEA:** You try out several lines you've read about: "Did it hurt when you fell from heaven? 'Cause you look like an angel to me!" They give a small smile and glance away. You go right to your next line: "Are your feet tired from running through my dreams all night?" They turn and glance around the room as if looking for someone. You try another one: "Do you work out? Because your abs are *abs*-olutely gorgeous!" Now they start walking away from you. You have one more line memorized: "If being beautiful were a crime, you should be arrested." Unfortunately, you have to deliver that one from the other side of a closed door. This did not go as planned.

✓ **BETTER IDEA:** You see them alone by the refreshment table, so you go over to them and introduce yourself. They introduce themself and ask you how you know the host. You tell them and ask the same question back. They notice you're wearing a T-shirt of your favorite band and start a conversation about it. You love talking about your music, and you loosen up and start talking more freely. You feel like the two of you are hitting it off, but you're not sure. You check in. Are you the only one doing the talking? If yes, it might be time to change the subject. If they're also talking about the band, you're probably okay. You're still not sure if they like you or they're just being nice, so you decide to ask. You say, "I don't like to assume too much when I'm getting to know someone new. I always hope that if someone likes me, they'll say so or give me their email address or something so I'll know if they want to continue the conversation." At this point, they might say, "Yeah, I know what you mean. Well, it was nice to meet you. See you around." Or they might say, "I feel the same way. Let me give you my email address, and maybe we can stay in touch." Either way, you have a pretty good idea of how they feel.

A COUPLE OF SINGLES

Bill

Bill hated social events, but sometimes he couldn't get out of it. His parents often had parties for their business associates, and since he lived there, he was expected to attend. Usually there were plenty of people his own age in attendance, and today was no different.

One young woman had a particularly piercing, high-pitched giggle. It seemed wherever he went, there she was. He went to get some refreshments and she was there, talking about how "yummy" everything looked and then giggling as if she had said something funny. He went to the bar for a drink, and she wanted him to make her something "sexy." What was that supposed to mean? Drinks

Chapter 2: Flirty or Friendly

are beverages; they're not sexy. Finally he went to the kitchen to get some more ice, and there she was again. She kept touching his arm, and every time she did, he jumped as if he had been shocked. Bill hated being unexpectedly touched, especially by someone he had just met.

At last he went out into the back yard, where a few guys were smoking cigarettes. Thank goodness she didn't follow him there. As much as he hated the smell of tobacco, he really needed to escape.

One of the guys said, "Hey, Danielle is really into you!"

"Who? What do you mean?" Bill looked around.

"Danielle, the girl who's been flirting with you all evening."

"She was flirting with me?"

"Yeah, and she's not very subtle, either. She must really be into you. Why don't you ask her out?"

Bill was stunned. A girl was flirting with him? He just thought she was annoying him for some unfathomable reason. Flirting?

"Don't you like her?"

Bill thought about it. "I don't know. I never thought about it. I guess she's cute. But her laugh is so annoying, I don't know if I could get beyond that."

"Dude, you should ask her out! Who cares about her laugh? You'll get used to it."

"I don't know. Maybe." But Bill knew it wasn't a Maybe; it was a No for him. He didn't want to even try to explain that the sound of her laughter was like a railroad spike being driven into his ear by John Henry. If that was flirting, then maybe flirting wasn't for him.

Trish

It was almost time for the department's regular ink and toner delivery. Trish kept checking her watch. She had been timing the deliveries for some time, and when she heard the delivery truck outside, she was ready to jump up and rush to the front desk. Once there, she didn't know what to do, so she started straightening and re-straightening the admissions pamphlets. Finally, he arrived and put the boxes on the counter. She wanted to say something. Why didn't she say something? What was all this planning for, if he was right here, and she didn't say anything at all?

"Well, hmm," she murmured.

"What?" He leaned toward her to hear better.

"Well, well, well, here we are." That was stupid. Now he would think she's stupid, and she's not. Except around him.

"Yep, here we are. And this is for you." He was holding something out toward her. Was he giving her something? This was unexpected.

"Um, what?"

"I need a signature. Right there." He held out the tablet, and she took it.

"My signature?" Why was she repeating things? Hadn't she planned something clever to say? What was it?

Chapter 2: Flirty or Friendly

"Yes, I need a signature that you received the delivery. You can use your finger."

"My finger?" Still repeating, like an idiot. She felt her face grow warm in embarrassment.

"Or the stylus. Whatever."

Trish signed shakily and handed the tablet back. She took a deep breath.

"I've enjoyed our time together today and hope that we will meet again in the future," she blurted out.

"Yeah, probably. This is my regular route." He touched the brim of his cap before turning away. "See you next time," he said as he left.

Well, she had done it. She had spoken to him. It was not at all the way she had planned it, but it was done now and there was no going back to change it. She had been ridiculous. But he hadn't laughed at her, so there was that. And the way he tapped his finger against his cap in farewell, almost like a tip of the hat, was charming.

Having spoken to him once, however disastrously, Trish felt encouraged. She might actually say something not stupid next delivery day. Time would tell.

ASK YOURSELF

How do you feel about flirting?

Some people are uncomfortable with subtleties and may miss it when someone tries to flirt. They may not realize someone is trying to let them know that they like them, assuming they were just being polite.

Others may try to flirt, but then it doesn't land the way they intended. Maybe they came on too strong and gave someone the wrong idea or scared them off. Maybe they were too low-key to be noticed, and the person they liked had no idea of how they felt.

Think about times you noticed that someone was flirting with you. What style of flirting makes you uncomfortable or puts you off? What kinds of flirting are fun for you and make you feel good? Maybe the best thing of all is if someone comes right out and tells you, in no uncertain terms, that they like you and might want to be more than just friends.

If you meet someone you find interesting and you'd like to get to know them better, consider using the kind of approach that you would appreciate the most if the situation were reversed. If you value straightforward, plain speech, then consider using it yourself. Many people like to create a script for a situation so they know what they're going to say in advance rather than ad-libbing. Having a good idea of what you want to say can

Chapter 2: Flirty or Friendly

make for clear communication. Ask yourself if this is the right choice for you.

ACTUALLY AUTISTIC LOVE STORIES

When I started dating my husband, I could tell immediately he was introverted, which was a relief. However, he was still NT and unlikely to do what I wished he would do: tell me exactly how he felt about me and our time together, with complete honesty and straight to the point. I have never enjoyed the subtle cues involved in dating and how difficult it can be to tell what somebody is really feeling. I knew we were hanging out a lot—which seemed good— and I was developing deep feelings for him. Yet, I had no idea how he felt since he would not verbally tell me. My friends told me to not ask him as it would be weird and too forward. I tried my very best but could not stand it anymore.

I finally went for it and told him exactly how I felt and was surprised when he stated he not only felt the same way but loved me.

— Ana, autism/ADHD, married to NT man

Dating While Autistic

When my husband and I met at a wedding reception, the minute I realized I liked him, I did everything I could not to let it show. I even ran and hid in the bathroom during the slow songs. I was convinced he was just being nice and passing the time by hanging out with me the whole night.

Even after a month of dating, I had to ask him, "Do you like me?"

His response was, "Um, of course. I'm crazy about you!"

Being undiagnosed at the time, I had no idea that what I needed was directness. Even a whole month of time invested together wasn't enough for me to know he actually cared about me more than just as a friend, because it was never directly stated. Flash forward a year later. He was acting strange, and he said some great things about me, followed by, "But this brings me to today." I was sure he was breaking up with me. No matter how complimentary his words were, all I could focus on was the word "But," which obviously negated all the nice things he'd said.

Imagine my surprise when he dropped to one knee and pulled out a ring to propose! I actually blurted out, "You're not breaking up with me?" before I accepted!

— Tara, autistic woman married to a man with ADHD

Chapter 3

How to Chat

Let's Talk About That

"Ideal conversation must be an exchange of thought, and not...an eloquent exhibition of wit or oratory."

— Emily Post

"There is no such thing as a worthless conversation, provided you know what to listen for. And questions are the breath of life for a conversation."

—James Nathan Miller

Chapter 3: How to Chat

Making conversation is one of the hardest things about dating for many people. Having to come up with casual comments to keep the conversational ball rolling does not always come naturally. So, what can you do to avoid long, awkward silences on your date?

Asking questions is the obvious solution. Just like rolling a ball back and forth between you, questions and answers can keep the chat moving. Making a list in advance of questions or topics of conversation is a good idea.

There is more to it than simply asking a series of questions, though. For instance, some people tend to talk quickly when they're nervous. They may rapidly ask a series of questions one after the other, barely even waiting for a reply. Their date might feel like they're being interrogated, which isn't pleasant. Imagine this scenario:

Person 1: What's your favorite food?

Person 2: Let's see, it's hard to choose just one, but I do like pizza.

P1: That's very interesting. What's your favorite drink?

P2: Well, I guess coffee, but I also like...

P1: That's very interesting. What's your favorite color?

P2: Um, blue?

P1: That's very interesting. What's your favorite TV show?

P2: ...I don't know, I don't have a TV.

P1: That's very interesting.

Dating While Autistic

As you can see, Person 1 has come up with a list of questions in order to have something to talk about but isn't giving Person 2 a chance to respond or really listening to them at all. It doesn't seem like much fun to be Person 2 on this date.

Instead of asking your list of questions one after the other, choose one question to ask first, listen to your date's response, and then see if they have a question for you. If they don't ask you something, you might give them your answer to the same question or find a way to build off of their response. Here's an example.

Person 1: Do you have a pet?

Person 2: Unfortunately, not right now, but I'd love to get a cat when I can.

P1: I love cats, I have two. Why can't you get one now?

P2: My landlord doesn't allow pets. My therapist thinks I should have one as a support animal, though, and we're working on that. What are your cats' names?

P1: I call them Sue and Gus, but their real names are Sushi and Asparagus.

P2: Cute! How did they get those names?

P1: They're named after the foods they try to steal. What's your favorite food?

P2: Let's see. It's hard to choose just one, but I do like pizza…

P1: I like pizza too, especially pepperoni. What kind of pizza do you like?

Chapter 3: How to Chat

P2:   I like plain cheese pizza, but if there's pepperoni, I don't mind. I just take them off.

P1:   I think they have pizza here. Shall we order a cheese and pepperoni pizza to share?

P2:   Good idea. Let's do that.

P1:   (while waiting for the pizza) Do you have a favorite TV show?

P2:   I don't have a TV.

P1:   Wow. What do you like to do instead of watching TV?

P2:   I watch YouTube on my phone.

P1:   I love YouTube! My favorite is watching otters.

P2:   My favorite is cats, but I like the otters, too. They're funny.

This time the conversation went much more smoothly. The person asking a question waited, listened to their date's answer, and then responded to what they heard before asking another question.

You may have heard people say that it's always a safe bet to talk about the weather, but unless there is some extreme weather going on at the moment or it's your partner's particular interest, weather is a pretty boring topic.

Another thing to avoid when asking questions getting too personal too quickly. For example, asking someone if they want to get married or have children or how much money they make is not a good idea during the early dating period. Your date might feel like you're pushing them to get serious too fast, or they might think you're only interested in their money. In the early stages of dating, it's fine to ask about someone's job or their family or your interests and hobbies. This is a time to get to know them as a person, hopefully to become friends, but not to interview them as a potential lover or spouse. Start slowly with casual conversation to learn about what kind of person they are rather than coming on too strong too fast.

What if your date is nervous and asks you too many questions too quickly? It's fine to ask for time to think about their question. You might repeat the question aloud and say, "That's a good question. Give me a minute to think about my answer." Pauses in conversation are okay, especially if you have acknowledged that you heard the question and that you are taking your time to process and give a thoughtful answer. Your date might be grateful for a moment of quiet between questions, too.

Here's a neurodivergent dating tip from Doug, who is married to Kelsey. Doug writes, "It's important to plan an activity that both you and your date are interested in. With an activity, you don't have to talk the entire time. If you want to go on a traditional dinner date, do so after the activity. That way, if there's a lull in the conversation, you can fall back on the shared experience that you both just had. Even a shared negative experience can generate a conversation. Just

Chapter 3: How to Chat

make sure to find out if your date agrees with you before sharing a strong negative opinion. You can do this by asking a question rather than making a statement in order to see where they stand. For example, when you don't know if your date liked the movie or not, try asking 'What did you think of the movie?' instead of saying, 'I thought that movie was stupid.'"

BAD IDEA/BETTER IDEA

You plan to meet someone for the first time on a blind date. Making conversation with someone new is not something you're good at. You're a bit nervous, and you worry that you won't know what to talk about.

✗ **BAD IDEA:** You arrange for your first date to be at a fancy restaurant. Once you get there, you sit awkwardly wondering what you're supposed to say. After talking about the weather, your date asks you what you like to do in your free time. Relieved for the invitation to talk about something you know a lot about, you spend the next forty minutes engaged in a monologue about your interest. By the end of the meal, she seems anxious to get away.

Dating While Autistic

✓ **BETTER IDEA:** After asking and learning what kinds of activities your date enjoys, the two of you arrange for your first date to include more than just sitting across a table looking at each other. You feel more comfortable sharing an activity, such as going for a walk in nature or going to a museum, convention, or zoo. The conversation flows naturally related to what you see and what is going on around you. By the end of your time together, you both have had fun and look forward to the next time.

A COUPLE OF SINGLES

Bill

Bill's parents arranged a blind date for him with Amber, the daughter of a couple in their social circle. He was nervous, but he also looked forward to it. Maybe this woman would be the one.

When Amber arrived at the restaurant, he stood abruptly, caught his water glass before it tipped over, and rushed forward to pull out her chair for her. There was an awkward moment when she stepped back and seemed startled, but then he pulled out her chair and gestured toward it. After she sat, he tried to push her chair in, but it was too heavy now that she was sitting on it, so he just went back to his place.

Chapter 3: How to Chat

"So, Amber, what do you do for a living?"

"I'm a database admin. What about you?"

"I'm a computer systems admin. Similar. I'm working from home, which is so much better."

"I'm back in the office. I really hated working from home. I'm glad to be back."

"Really?" Bill was surprised. "What was so bad about working from home?"

"I missed the people. It got lonely at home by myself all the time."

"Hmm. Well." Bill hesitated, and the silence seemed to stretch out too long. He had to say something, but what? "Which *Star Trek* series do you like best?"

"I don't know. I'm more of a *Star Wars* fan myself."

"*Star Wars*? Like with Jar Jar Binks? Seems ridiculous. The original *Star Trek* series was far superior, especially considering it in relation to other shows that aired in the same years. Don't you agree?"

"Like I said, I don't really know anything about *Star Trek*." Amber turned her attention to her menu. Bill knew he shouldn't keep talking about *Star Trek*, but the urge to tell her all the reasons why it was such a good show were bubbling up inside of him. He bit the inside of his cheek, jiggled his leg under the table, and took a deep breath. Then he picked up the menu. Although he had checked it out online and had already decided what he would order, he knew food would be a safer topic of conversation for him.

"So, have you been here before? What looks good?"

Amber had been there a few times and could recommend several items on the menu, including the one that Bill had already decided on. After they ordered, they chatted about their jobs while waiting for the food, and then talked about the food while they ate.

At the end of the evening, Bill wasn't sure if he wanted to see Amber again. He couldn't decide so quickly. They had things in common, like work, but he didn't know if he could date a *Star Wars* fan who had so little interest in *Star Trek*.

Three days later, he texted Amber and asked her if she wanted to go out again. She said she'd be happy to see him, but she wanted to be friends rather than dating. He felt hurt at first but then realized he wasn't really disappointed. He didn't have strong feelings for Amber; he just had strong feelings about wanting a woman in his life, and she had seemed nice enough. He decided to keep looking for the right person.

Trish

At the urging of one of her co-workers, Trish decided to try speed dating. She spent a long time getting ready, trying to make sure her hair and makeup were just right, and thinking of the questions she would ask her dates. She knew she wanted to get married and

Chapter 3: How to Chat

have children of her own someday. It was important to her that her children would one day go to the college where her parents met and fell in love, where she herself had attended for four years, and where she still worked. She loved working in admissions and thinking of the eager high school students whose applications passed through her hands on their way to being (she hoped) accepted for admission.

When she took her seat at the small table waiting for her first speed date to arrive, she went over in her mind the questions she had prepared. (1) Where did you go to college? (2) Are you familiar with my college? (3) Where do you want your children to go to college? (4) How many children do you want to have?

She asked each date these questions, and their responses seemed to be lukewarm at best. By the time she got to her fourth question, they were looking at their watch and glancing over their shoulders, clearly bored and anxious to move on.

The questions they asked her all seemed to be related to physical outdoor activities. Did she like to hike or ski or camp or watch sports? She did not like any of those things and told them so.

After the speed dating experience, she was hard-pressed to find anyone to check off on her list indicating she would like to see them again. Finally she put a check mark next to the one who had the cutest hair, even though he loved going camping and she hated it. She was not really surprised when she didn't get a match to follow up on. Although she was disappointed in the experience, she wasn't disappointed that those men didn't want to date her again. The feeling was mutual. Maybe next time she would rewrite her questions to focus on the present rather than on the future, like how many children they wanted. She wouldn't rush off in that direction but would try to find someone who liked reading and attending lectures and going to the movies when it wasn't crowded. Surely there were men out there who liked the same kinds of things that she liked, and one day she would find one.

ASK YOURSELF

How do you feel about answering questions? Many people find it stressful, but it can be a great way to get to know someone better. What would make the process of getting to know each other easier for you? For many, knowing in advance what questions they might be asked helps a lot. Perhaps you and your date can each think of three questions you'd like to ask each other. You can send them by email or text in advance and have time to think about your answers. When you meet, you'll already know how the conversation will start. Ask yourself whether this might not get your next first date conversation off to a good start.

Chapter 3: How to Chat

ACTUALLY AUTISTIC LOVE STORIES

My husband, Elliot, and I met on OkCupid. I'd been using the app for a few months, but when I saw Elliot's profile, I just knew. It was so HONEST. He wasn't trying to be impressive or act like someone he wasn't. He listed "tide pooling" and "LEGO®" as two of his interests.

On our second date, we talked for hours about every issue we could think of. We didn't want to play games; we were clear about what we wanted. After years of trying to pretend I was the "cool girl," it was so refreshing to say, "Actually, I do want a serious relationship. I do want marriage. I do want kids." We laid out our politics and our beliefs, and the result is that we never had to play a single game.

— Marian

Chapter 4

Respect Boundaries

Don't Overstep, and Don't Get Stepped Over

"Daring to set boundaries is about having the courage to love ourselves, even when we risk disappointing others."

— Brene Brown

"I learned a long time ago the wisest thing I can do is be on my own side, be an advocate for myself and others like me."

— Maya Angelou

Chapter 4: Respect Boundaries

A boundary is anything that makes a border. On maps, lines dividing nations and regions are drawn in, although you can't see them if you're flying in an airplane. But these invisible boundaries can be just as important as if each one were marked by a Great Wall.

Boundaries between people are also invisible and just as important. In dating, if you don't know where the boundaries are, it's easy to get into trouble.

Overstepping someone's boundaries, even without realizing you're doing it, can lead to making them uncomfortable, angry, or even fearful enough to call 911.

You might like someone and want to go out with them, hoping someday to have a romantic relationship. People in relationships know where their partner lives, and you don't know where the object of your affection lives. It seems logical to you that you should find out, so you follow them home and stand outside, looking up. In your head you're hearing the song "On the Street Where You Live" from *My Fair Lady*. Just like Freddy in that musical, you're happy just to be on the street, near your crush, with no desire to go further. Unfortunately, to the person you've followed, you appear to be stalking them. They may decide you're creepy, potentially dangerous. At best, they might feel extremely uncomfortable and actively avoid you in the future. At worst, they might call the police.

Dating While Autistic

Either way, following someone is overstepping their boundary, and it's never okay.

Another way people overstep boundaries without meaning to is by asking personal questions. If you work or go to school with someone and you want to get to know them better, don't start off by coming on too strong. Don't ask if they are single, or if they want to have children someday, or how much money they make. Don't ask for their personal email or phone number.

If you ask about their interests or what book they're reading or what shows they're watching, or if you comment on something you two share such as work or school, you can be pretty sure you're not stepping over any personal boundaries. It takes time and patience for a friendship to develop, and pushing too hard or fast can stop it before it starts.

This goes both ways, of course. If someone else oversteps your personal boundaries and you don't put a stop to it early, you might find yourself in a situation you don't want to be in with no clear way out. It's especially important to be wary of new people if you tend to be smaller or weaker than them. Sometimes a friendly tone is misinterpreted as flirtatious, and someone can get the wrong idea. If you don't notice that the person you're talking to is moving closer, if you find yourself alone with them, especially if you feel cornered, you could be in trouble. Be aware of your surroundings and their proximity. Don't be shy about saying,

Chapter 4: Respect Boundaries

"You're too close; please back up." If someone asks you very personal questions, like if you live alone, or details about your past relationships, this could be a danger sign. Just because someone asks a question, you are not obligated to answer. You can ignore it, change the subject, or say right out, "I'm not comfortable talking about things like that." Move away if you feel cornered, and find other people if you are alone with someone you don't know well. Even if they have the best of intentions, you get to delineate your own boundaries. No one has the right to overstep and make you uncomfortable.

Boundaries are not only physical, like getting too close or trying to move from a platonic to a romantic relationship too quickly. How often someone wants to communicate, whether by text, email, or phone, is another boundary. One person might feel it's fun to text someone a regular good morning and good night, with other cheerful gifs and texts sprinkled throughout the day. They should first be sure those communications are welcome. Someone else might not want to text daily and might feel smothered. It's okay to ask how often they like to get a text and what times of day are best. Some people like to text their date goodnight before they fall asleep. For others, the idea of getting a text late at night when they're probably already in bed feels too intimate, even if what is said is not particularly sexual. Find out what the other person wants, and then stick to their preferences.

Dating While Autistic

Everyone's boundaries are different. There are no hard and fast rules, except to go slowly enough to become aware of a boundary before you discover you've already crossed it. Put yourself in the other person's shoes and try to see things from their perspective to help figure out where their boundaries are. When in doubt, let them know that you don't want to overstep, and ask them about boundaries.

BAD IDEA/BETTER IDEA

You've had a very enjoyable first date with someone you met online. The two of you have shared a good meal and a walk, and found things to chat and laugh about together. You feel very comfortable in their company and hope this is the beginning of something special and long term. Now you've walked back to the parking lot and are standing by their car, ready to say good night.

✘ **BAD IDEA:** You've seen plenty of movies and TV shows with couples on dates. Usually at the end of the date, they share a passionate kiss up against a wall. You feel like this is the right time for a kiss, and there's no wall, but their car is right here. You move forward, pressing your date against their car door, and lean in for a big kiss. That's when you get pushed away

Chapter 4: Respect Boundaries

roughly, and they leap into their car, slam and lock the door, and peel out at top speed. That did not go as you expected.

✓ **BETTER IDEA:** You feel like a goodnight kiss would be the perfect ending to a lovely evening. But does your date feel the same way? You realize not everyone feels comfortable kissing on the first date. What would be appropriate? A hug? A handshake? As you stand together by their car, you decide it's best to just ask. It might sound awkward, but an awkward question is better than an awkward attempt at a hug or kiss if it's not reciprocated. You take a deep breath and go for it, saying something like, "I've really enjoyed spending time with you. How do you feel about a hug or a handshake?" Then you listen and respect your date's preference. Whether you two end up hugging, shaking hands, or just waving goodbye, you both know that the choice was made together, with the greatest respect for boundaries. Respect is a good beginning to any friendship or relationship.

Dating While Autistic

A COUPLE OF SINGLES

Bill

At the urging of a friend, Bill signed up for a speed dating experience. He figured, what did he have to lose? He showed up at the event in a suit and tie and felt a bit overdressed but decided not to worry about it. The coordinator, Heather, was friendly, and he felt immediately comfortable with her. She seemed so cheerful and welcoming, and he was glad he came.

As he went from table to table during the event, though, his comfort level plummeted. Each woman seemed lackluster in comparison with Heather. They looked as nervous as he felt, and two nervous people together was not a great recipe for success. Some of them told him how great he looked in his suit and asked him about his job and what kind of car he drove. They seemed more interested in money and prestige than they were in him. Others took one look at him and then glanced at their watch or at the man at the next table that they would talk to after Bill. Everything seemed so rushed, and he couldn't keep track of who said what.

The bottom line was no one clicked. There was not a single woman there that he had any interest in seeing again.

Except Heather.

In the short time he spent with Heather as she explained the speed dating rules and procedures, he felt a solid connection. She

Chapter 4: Respect Boundaries

made him feel comfortable. Not just comfortable, but confident. Bill felt like a winner when she was smiling at him, and he didn't often feel like a winner. She was something special.

He looked over all the names on his form and didn't check a box by any of his speed dates. Instead, he wrote in Heather's name and added that she was the only one he was interested in dating. With slightly trembling hands, he gave her his form and quickly left the room before she could read it. Excitement bubbled up inside him as he thought about her response. Clearly, she felt the same way; he could tell by the way she smiled at him. This was the beginning of something wonderful.

Only it wasn't.

He waited for the call that all participants were promised, where Heather would tell them which women they'd matched with and share contact information. Since he had only selected one woman, he knew whose phone number he would be getting. He waited for her call, but it didn't come all day. The next day, and the day after that, still nothing. Bill started to worry. Had he been he wrong to write in Heather's name? True, she wasn't one of the speed daters, but he had definitely felt a connection. Surely she felt it, too?

After a week, he tried calling the number he had for the speed dating service, and when no one answered, he left a message. He wasn't even sure what he said, because he was feeling emotional about not hearing back from her to set up a date. No return call. Finally, he went back to the speed dating website and tried to book another session, only to find that he had been blocked. He was shocked, hurt, and embarrassed. He had been so sure that she liked him, based on how friendly she was and how she put him at ease.

But maybe she did that with everyone. It finally dawned on him that it was her job to make everyone feel comfortable and relaxed. Like a waitress who smiles at you because it's her job, and maybe because smiling means a better tip. Just because a waitress is friendly and attentive, it doesn't mean she wants to be friends, and Heather's job was kind of the same. She was supposed to help people feel confident and happy to be there so that their speed dating experience would be positive.

He had blown it. Bill was down about it for several days, and embarrassed. He replayed their conversation over and over in his head and felt worse about his response each time.

Finally, he knew he had to stop. So what if he had gotten the wrong idea with Heather? She was probably used to it and had forgotten all about it by then. He had learned that speed dating was not for him, anyway, because of the fast pace of meeting new people. That was good to know. But he really needed to shake off intruding memories of his "speed dating disaster."

Bill came up with a plan. Every time he started to ruminate about how he had made a fool of himself with Heather, he

Chapter 4: Respect Boundaries

mentally told himself, "Stop. The past doesn't matter. Look ahead!" He even made a sticky note to put on his bathroom mirror to remind him.

Eventually, he spent less and less time thinking about the past and more time enjoying the present and looking forward to a happier future. Stopping unwanted thoughts by talking back to them helped Bill move on.

Trish

During the days between deliveries, Trish couldn't stop thinking about the delivery man who had tipped his hat to her so charmingly. She pictured his face every day. Doing so made her realize he was probably younger than she was. How much younger? She couldn't be sure. Did young men like to date older women? How would she know? She knew nothing about men of any age. She would have to do some research. Who might know what young men like? A young man, of course.

There was a student intern who worked part time in admissions, a young man named … Anthony? Adam? That sounded right. She could ask Adam next time he was in the office.

The next day was his regular shift, and Trish was ready for him.

"Good morning, Adam," she said. She remembered to smile and look towards his face, because people like it when you did that.

"Uh, it's Aiden." Oops.

Dating While Autistic

"Yes, Aiden. Good morning, Aiden." She kept smiling and looking his way. What else should she say?

"Good morning, I guess." He started sorting the mail.

"I wonder if you could help me with something," she said.

"Sure, that's my job."

"Can you tell me if young men like to date older women?"

"I guess some of them do. What do you mean?"

"I mean someone my age. Do you think a young man would want to have a relationship with someone my age?" She didn't like to look right at his eyes, so she looked at his mouth instead.

"Whoa. I never thought about it." He was staring at her now, and he started smiling too. "I mean, yeah, sure, a young man would love that. Wow. This is really unexpected, but, oh my god, yes!" He put down the mail and came over closer to her. "So, should we go to your place?"

"Why would we go to my place?" Trish was confused now. It was good to know that someone as young as the delivery guy might want to date her, but what was this intern talking about?

"Well, you know, I live in the dorm, so we can't go there. Unless you're into it. I mean, I could put a sock on the doorknob so my roommate won't interrupt us. Whatever you're into, I'm up for it." He was standing really close to her now, and he put his hand on her arm.

Chapter 4: Respect Boundaries

Trish jumped backward and moved quickly to the other side of the counter. "No! Stop that! Don't touch me!" She couldn't believe this was happening. "I do not date students! You misunderstand me!"

Aiden's face turned red, and he backed away. "Wow, I don't believe you. You were coming on to me, and now you're all—" He turned to leave, and shouted over his shoulder, "You're crazy, lady!" Then he was gone.

Trish went to hide in the ladies' room, where no one could see her rock and flap her hands and cry. She was humiliated. All she wanted was to gather data on young men in general, and that boy thought she was propositioning him! Was she guilty of sexual harassment? That was so far from her intention, but looking back at the conversation, she realized it could be seen that way. She could be fired for this!

Trish took a couple of days off as sick days, since she had them coming and she really did feel sick about what happened. She got no phone call from HR asking her to come in for a reprimand or requiring her to re-take the sexual harassment training. What had Aiden said about what happened? Who had he told?

When she got back to work, she learned that Aiden had requested a transfer to another department, and the request was granted. No one knew, or seemed to care, why he wanted the transfer. Trish was so relieved, she almost cried. Then she went to the ladies' room so she could cry, letting out all of her pent-up fear and anxiety. From now on, she would think very carefully about what she said before she said it. Looking at something from the other person's perspective might keep her from a repeat of this week's catastrophe. A new week, a new opportunity, and a more thoughtful, careful attitude. Trish was going to be okay.

ASK YOURSELF

Do you know how to advocate for yourself if someone tries to overstep your boundaries? It's difficult, isn't it? That's an uncomfortable conversation to start with, but often there's the added stress of being unsure about what happened. Did they really mean anything by it? Were you just overreacting?

Never keep quiet when someone makes you uncomfortable by overstepping your comfort zone. It doesn't matter if it seems reasonable to someone else. If you feel pushed or cornered or confused about someone's intentions, you have a right to say so.

This is particularly important if someone has repeatedly made you uncomfortable and hasn't picked up on your hints that you don't like their behavior. Consider creating a script for yourself and practicing in front of the mirror so that you are prepared the next time it happens. Speak up and tell them you don't like what they're

Chapter 4: Respect Boundaries

doing or how they're treating you. You deserve to be heard, and no one has the right to cross your boundaries.

And how much better will you feel after you tell them how you really feel?

ACTUALLY AUTISTIC LOVE STORIES

We met at work! I (Aym) had been working at this restaurant for several years, and Brenna got hired. Neither of us knew we were autistic at the time, and neither of us was looking for any sort of serious romantic relationship.

Our immediate deep connection was a surprise to us both. Each of us felt seen and understood in a way we never thought possible. It felt like a fairy tale.

Meeting each other and falling in love was both of us unmasking for the first time. We didn't think it was possible to be understood and loved and accepted. There was a lot of fear at first, being so vulnerable and exposed, but it was an exciting fear—if we were afraid of what we could lose, that meant there was so much more to gain.

— Aym and Brenna

Chapter 5

Sense & Sensory Sensibility

It's Different for Everyone

"Sensory issues ... make it impossible to operate in the environment where you're supposed to be social."

— Dr. Temple Grandin

"I go to nature to be soothed and healed, and to have my senses put in order."

— John Burroughs

Chapter 5: Sense & Sensory Sensibility

People are always looking for things they have in common with someone they want to date. Commonalities bind people together and increase understanding.

One thing many autistic people have in common is unusual or extreme responses to sensory experiences. This commonality is not something to base a relationship on alone, but it is something to be mindful of. Sharing sensory responses can be a good thing and can help two people understand each other.

If both partners hate loud noises, neither of them will try to arrange to go to rock concerts together. If they both love the smell of lavender, an excursion to a local lavender farm would be welcome. These shared preferences enhance compatibility.

It's when your sensory needs and preferences are different that you need to be mindful. Before suggesting a date at a casino, for example, find out how they feel about bright lights, loud music, crowds, and smoke. If they don't share your interest in casinos, it could be a disaster of a first date.

On your first meeting, try playing the "Love/Not" game. In this game you take turns listing one thing you Love, and one thing you do Not love. Remember, just one Love and one Not per round, so it doesn't turn into a laundry list.

You could take turns choosing topics for each round. For instance, if the topic is Foods, one partner might say "I Love crispy hash browns but Not mushy mashed potatoes." For clothing, someone might say, "I Love tagless T-shirts but Not turtlenecks." For places to go on a date, you might tell your partner, "I Love eating in a restaurant overlooking the ocean but Not walking on the sandy beach." Someone might say, "I Love having music playing while we eat but Not hearing someone chew their food." Each of you shares your "Love/Not" ideas, and you see where you overlap. Do both of you Love museums but Not movie theaters, or Love a walk in the park but Not a stroll through a mall? Together you can find things you both enjoy doing and make plans to do one of them on your next date.

It's important to be aware of things your date doesn't like. If they have scent sensitivities, don't wear perfume or cologne on your date. If stripes give them a headache, wear a solid color. Remembering their preferences is a sign of respect.

It's also important for you to let them know if there are experiences that are particularly painful for you. If the sound of denim fabric being brushed or rubbed together makes your stomach hurt and brings on a migraine, it would be a kindness if your date would avoid wearing denim jeans on your date. If the sight of rhubarb makes you nauseated and you notice rhubarb pie on the menu, it's okay to tell your date. If they know, they might decide to choose a different pie instead of rhubarb when the two of you are on a date.

Don't make a long list of everything in the world that could possibly bother you and present it, or you might scare them away.

Chapter 5: Sense & Sensory Sensibility

How can they hope to have a relationship with someone who has so many rules? Limit it to the thing that would be a dealbreaker for you, such as an allergy or extreme reaction, and see how your date feels about it. If they say they adore rhubarb so whenever they see it on the menu they simply have to order it, or their favorite outfit is denim and it gives them comfort or confidence to wear it, maybe you two are not right for each other. However, many sensory issues might be a "small deal," and these can often be accommodated without big problems.

Remember, it goes both ways. Ask your date if there are sensory experiences that are dealbreakers for them, and then do your best to avoid the things that you know will be distressing to them. Together you can approach unique sensory responses with open communication and mutual respect.

Here's a sensory tip from Kelsey, who's married to Doug. Kelsey writes, "My husband, Doug, likes to listen to TV at a loud volume, but I have sensitive ears. Sometimes I can tolerate loud TV for a while, but other times I must politely ask him to turn it down. It helped to have a discussion about our sensory needs, since we found that he is particularly sensitive just before bed, and my sensitivity can vary throughout the day. He bought wireless noise-canceling headphones that we can each use when we need peace and quiet."

Dating While Autistic

BAD IDEA/BETTER IDEA

You're on your first dinner date with a new friend. You like them and want to make a good impression, hoping that someday you might be more than friends. Your date asks if you mind if they order fish, and you say of course, no problem. You've never minded if someone eats fish and chips near you.

Then they order the salmon, and you remember that while most fish smells don't bother you, the smell of salmon is something you find almost intolerable. But you already said it was fine to order fish.

What should you do?

✗ **BAD IDEA:** You don't say anything, since you already told them to go ahead and order fish. Maybe it won't be so bad. When the waiter brings the food, you realize it is bad. The smell is horrible. You try holding your napkin in front of your nose to block it, but it doesn't work. Every time you inhale, you feel like you're choking. You drink as much water as you can, and when you run out of water, you quickly down your cocktail. Now you feel ill. You run to the restroom and hope your date can't tell that you've been vomiting. You feel so miserable you can't carry on a conversation, and the evening ends in awkward silence.

Chapter 5: Sense & Sensory Sensibility

✓ **BETTER IDEA:** You realize that you made a mistake and jump in to correct it, saying, "I'm so sorry, I said that I'm fine with ordering fish, but I forgot that I have a bad reaction to the smell of salmon. Any other fish is fine. I hope you can find something else to order that you would enjoy as much."

Your date says, "Oh, of course, I understand, no problem. I'll have the hazelnut encrusted sole instead, it looks good."

The rest of the evening goes smoothly because you admitted your mistake and advocated for yourself.

A COUPLE OF SINGLES

Bill

Bill scheduled a session with a neurodivergent dating coach who arranged a blind date for him with an autistic woman his age. It seemed like a good idea, since they wouldn't have to try to explain their neurodivergence. Dating another autistic person would be a great opportunity to relax and not have to mask or try to act "normal" for the evening.

They met at a restaurant, and although they were both nervous, they seemed to hit it off pretty well. After their food arrived, Bill noticed that his date would periodically wince, squeezing her eyes shut and pressing her lips together. At first he brushed it off as a stim, but it went on and she didn't look happy. Wasn't the purpose of a stim to relax you or reduce stress?

Finally he asked her what was wrong. At first she shook her head rapidly and said, "Nothing, everything's fine." But she didn't look fine.

"Please, tell me what it is. If I'm doing something wrong, I want to know."

She took a deep breath and looked down, speaking quietly. "It's the way you eat. Every time you take a bite, you scrape your fork against your teeth when you pull it back out of your mouth. That scraping sound makes my skin crawl, and I don't know how long I can take it. I'm sorry."

"No, I'm sorry. I had no idea I was doing that. I can stop," Bill said. But could he stop? He had never thought about how he ate. Could he change? After the next bite he slowly pulled the fork out through his lips without letting it touch his teeth. His date smiled and thanked him. He tried it again on the next bite. This was manageable, and it seemed like an easy thing to change since it was obviously so important to his date.

They started talking about their interests, and Bill thought everything was going great until he saw her wince. Uh, oh, he'd done the scraping thing again. He had to think about every bite now. Was he keeping the fork well away from his teeth? Apparently, he could either focus on how he was eating

Chapter 5: Sense & Sensory Sensibility

or he could make conversation, but he couldn't do both at the same time.

Before long he quit trying to eat. He asked for a to-go container for the rest of his dinner and ate it as soon as he got home.

Bill considered asking her for a second date, but the thought exhausted him.

Trish

Trish had been feeling so down in the dumps that she decided to finally say "Yes" and join her co-workers the next Friday night. They went to a club with dancing and free appetizers, and everyone seemed to have a good time. One by one the others were invited to dance, and Trish volunteered to stay at the booth and watch their purses. This was her comfort level, watching them dance and enjoy the music. She had put some earbuds into her ears, not connected to any music, but to block out some of the noise. It looked like the whole clubbing experience might not be as bad as she feared.

Then the unthinkable happened.

A man in the next booth was asking her to dance. A strange man. She hadn't even considered this possibility, so at first she froze. Apparently he thought she hadn't heard him, so he got up, came around to stand in front of her, and repeated, "I said, would you like to dance?" Now she couldn't ignore him. What could she do? She didn't have a script or tool in her social toolbox to deal with the problem of Strange Man Asking for a Dance.

Then she had a thought. He had assumed she couldn't hear him. What if she really couldn't? What if he thought she was deaf? She remembered a summer school course in American Sign Language, and signed, "No thank you." Then she looked down at her drink and waited for him to go away. Unfortunately, thinking she was deaf did not make him go away; it seemed to make him try harder. He was gesturing, pointing to the dance floor, making his fingers act out dancing in a sort of pantomime. Why didn't he give up and leave her alone? She kept shaking her head, signing "No," and refusing to look at him until at last he gave up and wandered off to ask someone else to dance.

The flashing lights, the booming bass that no earbuds could block, the cacophony of raised voices trying to carry on countless conversations, and the smell of fruity drinks and fried food suddenly made her feel incredibly ill. The social stress of having a stranger talk to her now made it impossible for her to ignore the sensory nightmare.

As soon as one of her co-workers came back to the table so she could relinquish her purse-watching duties, Trish called a car and went home. Never again! The club scene was not for her.

Chapter 5: Sense & Sensory Sensibility

ASK YOURSELF

What sensory experiences are the most difficult for you to cope with? Think about the sounds, or textures that set your teeth on edge, or the kind of lighting that gives you a headache, or the smells or foods that nauseate you. Make a list, and then rank them from the most obnoxious to the more bearable. Are there some that could be accommodated or made more manageable with supports such as earplugs for noise or dark glasses for lights? For unexpected odors like cleaning products or chemical perfumes, would it help to carry something that smells good to you, a few coffee beans, or a lavender sachet to sniff if you've been exposed to the noxious smell?

Next to each item on your list, make a note of whether you can do something to make it easier for you to cope with. Then you can have a better idea of what sensory things would be a dealbreaker for you and which might be negotiable.

However, if someone tells you that you need to go through some kind of desensitization process for your sensory dealbreakers, you can respectfully decline. No one else has the right to tell you that you have to get used to sensory experiences to make life easier or more comfortable for other people.

If you decide for yourself that one of your sensory nightmares could be reduced, talk to your counselor or medical provider. Adding things like earplugs or broad-brimmed hats might be sufficient. No one should undertake sensory desensitization except professionals who have been trained in its use, and even if you do decide to start such a program with a professional, you have the right to stop it at any time.

Now, what about the sensory experiences that you find the most pleasing, or calming, or delightful? Make a list of these. Maybe you love the sound of drums, or the smell of roses, or the sight of light reflecting off the surface of water, or the feeling of squishable plush, or the taste of dark chocolate or red wine. Write down all of the sensory things that bring you joy. Which of these might lend itself to a first-date activity? A walk through a rose garden, lunch beside a lake, a wine-tasting event, or even a trip to a store that allows you to build your own plush toy. There is no age limit on fun, as long as both of you enjoy the same kind of fun. So, share some of these ideas with your date, and ask: What kinds of sensory experiences are the most fun for you?

ACTUALLY AUTISTIC LOVE STORIES

When Elliot and I first got married, I worked at a hip tech company with an open plan office in downtown San Francisco. Open plan did not work for me. By 11 AM, I was completely spent, unable to do anything except stare at the computer and wait for the day to

Chapter 5: Sense & Sensory Sensibility

end. I'd go into the bathroom and sit with my back pressed against the cool tile or put rain music on my headphones and practice deep breathing.

Nothing helped.

At 5 PM, I'd drive the hour home and crawl into bed. Elliot would arrive to find me wrapped up in a blanket burrito.

"Do you want me to lie on you?" he'd ask.

"Yes please."

I'd open up the blanket and unfurl myself and he'd lay his whole body weight on top of me. The air would rush out of my lungs in one big heave, and with it the open plan office and the fluorescent lights and the honking cars and the constant conversation and the traffic. The itchy feeling along my skin that had grown and spread all day was snuffed out. I felt safe again and just a little more functional.

— Marian

Chapter 6

Interests

Yours, Mine, and Ours

"If a guy can't handle it when you talk about quantum physics, manga, or Dungeons & Dragons, then he probably isn't the guy for you."

— Rudy Simone, *Aspergirls*

"Our interests allow us to decompress, calm down, focus our energy, and give us a reason to be excited about life—a purpose."

— Jeannie Davide-Rivera, author of *Twirling Naked in the Streets and No One Noticed: Growing Up With Undiagnosed Autism*

Chapter 6: Interests

E veryone has interests. Some people have typical interests shared by many, such as being interested in music or nature. Some have specific interests, such as learning all they can about a particular band from the 1980s or about wild mushrooms of the Pacific Northwest. Some people are mildly interested in many things, and others are intensely, deeply interested in one or two things. But the fact that you have interests is something you share with all of humanity.

If you have a specific, intense interest, you may want to date someone who shares, or at least understands, your passion. You don't have to have identical hobbies in order to have a good relationship, but you should each have an understanding of and respect for your date's special interests or "spins."

If you look for a date in the usual places, such as going to dating sites, bars, or speed dating events, it is not too likely you'll happen to run into someone who shares your "spin." However, no matter how specific and obscure your interest is, be assured you're not the only person who shares that passion. If you search online, you will find people and groups devoted to collecting the same things you collect.

For instance, if you love knitting, scenic city views, and carousels, you might want to check out Scenic Stitches in DUMBO. People meet up for a lovely afternoon knitting near a carousel with stunning views of Manhattan. If you were hoping for a Disney connection, you'll be disappointed, though, because the DUMBO in this case stands for Down Under Manhattan Bridge Overpass. Bridge enthusiasts will be interested. Of course, for the Disney fans, it is easy to find groups of people who share your devotion to Disney at the touch of a computer mouse.

If you love to learn about your interest, find courses where you'll meet others who want to learn about the same things, whether you're learning Japanese, drawing, martial arts, French cooking, writing, making sushi, or regency dancing.

The important thing to remember is that you don't need to have identical interests in order to enjoy dating someone. You do need to respect your date's interests and listen to them talk about what they love for at least as much time as you talk about your passions. Nobody wants to feel trapped in a two-hour private TED talk they didn't sign up for.

Remember to take turns, respond to what your date says, and check in regularly while you're talking. If you see signs that you're over-sharing, if they keep glancing at the time or looking around the room, then perhaps it's time for you to stop talking and ask them a question about their interests. It can be difficult to stop when you're on a roll, so plan a strategy for yourself. Consider carrying a small stone or fidget object in your pocket and when it's time to listen, take it out and hold it while your date talks. Perhaps you'd find it helpful to bring a card with a list of questions you could ask your

Chapter 6: Interests

date. My own parents met as shy teenagers. Before their first date, my mother wrote down a list of topics she thought would help get the conversation started. When she arrived at the date, she realized she had forgotten the list at home. Admitting that broke the ice and became their first topic of conversation. That first awkward, shy date led to a happy marriage lasting over half a century.

BAD IDEA/BETTER IDEA

You are a devoted fan of a classic fantasy trilogy written in the 1930s and 1940s. A friend has arranged a blind date for you with someone they say has similar interests to yours. You are excited to meet this person and discuss your favorite books. When you meet, you realize your date knows little about your beloved trilogy but is a huge fan of a modern-day magical fantasy. Although you suppose the books are well-written, you have no respect for the author, whose political beliefs are vastly different from your own. What do you do?

✗ **BAD IDEA:** You tell your date that the author they love is a horrible person. You recount all the various ways in which they are a horrible person. You bring out your phone to look up their hateful tweets to prove your point. When you finally find the tweets you were looking for, you realize your date has left. They didn't even wait for the food to arrive. You never see them again.

✓ **BETTER IDEA:** You cringe inwardly when you think of all the horrible things that author has said and written, things you cannot abide. You realize your date loves this author and would not welcome you going off on them. Instead, you say that you know the author is talented but that you have some important differences in beliefs and values. You share that you're the kind of person who can't set aside your feelings about the author's statements from their work, so you have chosen not to read their books. Then you change the subject to something not controversial, like asking about your date's work, or hobbies, or what television shows they love. At the end of the date, you realize you were able to have a pleasant time together in spite of your different interests. You may or may not be able to put your strong feelings aside to go forward with a second date, but at least you made it through the evening without offense or argument.

Chapter 6: Interests

A COUPLE OF SINGLES

Bill

After the fiasco with the date from *Star Wars*, Bill decided the way to find a date who shared his interest was by going to a *Star Trek* convention. There was one fairly near him, so he bought his ticket and made his plans. He researched everything about the convention, from parking to food to a map of the center so he could see where the restrooms were located. He made calendar appointments on his phone for every breakout room class, lecture, and autograph or photo opportunity event that interested him so that an alarm would notify him in time. He didn't want to get so caught up browsing in the vendor's hall that he missed something he'd been looking forward to.

On the day of the convention, he paid close attention to detail in his cosplay. He was going dressed as the original Captain Kirk, season 1, episode 28, "The City on the Edge of Forever." He looked again at the image from the episode online. Yes. Everything was perfect.

When he arrived, he was prepared for the crowds and the noise. He had earplugs in and kept to the perimeters rather than being right in the middle of everything. He was aware of where every restroom and every exit were located, in case he needed a break from the overwhelming event.

Dating While Autistic

One of the events he didn't want to miss was a discussion about the original series. That was his favorite. There had been many spin-offs and movies, but the original had a certain nostalgic element that had always appealed to him. When he got to the room, he noticed that everyone else there was his parents' age. Not one woman he would consider "datable." Of course, these were the people who had seen the original series when it first aired, back in the sixties. Nice to know they were still fans, but it was disappointing not to find anyone his age who appreciated the classic style of the original.

The old guy he sat next to was wearing a red *Star Trek* shirt, and his name tag said, "Don't bother with my name, I won't be around long." Bill chuckled, recognizing the joke. In the original series, whenever they beamed down to a planet, it was always the nameless guys in red shirts who died first.

The old guy noticed him laughing and nodded. "You get it. Most people your age don't."

"I know. People keep asking me why I didn't wear a costume. I tell them I'm Captain Kirk, but they don't believe me."

"Of course, I see it. The red and black plaid shirt, blue jeans, it's one of the time travel episodes."

"Yes! When he fell in love and had to watch her die."

The old guy's wife chimed in. "That was always my favorite episode. It was so sweet and so sad." Her husband patted her hand

Chapter 6: Interests

and they smiled at each other. Bill wished he could be like that old couple someday. He'd love to have a wife who shared his interests, someone to be by his side. Even though there was no one his age in this particular group, meeting this couple gave him hope.

Someday, he too would find his perfect match, and together they would boldly go forth into the future.

Trish

Trish decided to go to her ten-year college homecoming reunion. She hated the idea of reunions as a rule and hadn't had a lot of friends in college, but she did have happy memories of those days. She had been a literature major, focusing on historical science fiction, and the days spent in the college library were precious. Plus, her college was a special interest of hers, and this reunion was a chance to experience another aspect of college life.

Because she was also a college employee, she volunteered to set up and manage the registration table. Having a job to do gave her the anchor she needed. She could socialize briefly with people who came to get checked in and to pick up their name tags, but then they moved on. It was easy for her to use the same script with each person who came to her table, and she didn't have the chance to run out of things to say. Since her table was out in the hall, she was spared the loud music, bright lights, and pushing crowd. Talking to one person at a time, with a specific goal for the interaction, was exactly in her comfort zone.

At the end of the evening, she hadn't made any kind of personal connection with anyone, but that was okay. She had been among people her age and had recognized a few of them from classes they had shared, and she had been useful and not awkward. For Trish, this social event was a win.

ASK YOURSELF

What are your favorite interests? How many other interests can you think of that might overlap with yours? Your date may or may not share your interest exactly, but there are so many overlapping and associated interests that a perfect match might not be necessary. Remember the last time you dove down a rabbit hole researching your passion. Did you see all those other possible directions your dive might have followed? Maybe your date followed a parallel path. What might you learn from them about their interests?

Chapter 6: Interests

ACTUALLY AUTISTIC LOVE STORIES

We do share some interests, like watching TV or movies together, but our big interests are not shared. Brenna loves playing video games, and I love photography/graphic design. So we have "separate together" time, just hanging out in the same space doing our own interests quietly near each other.

Whenever one of us has something we want to show the other (like a cool picture or new thing in a game), we ask, "Hey, can I show you something?" We give the other person an opportunity to take a minute to ready their brain for incoming stimuli. We have learned over the years to communicate very clearly and set expectations to try and minimize getting overstimulated.

— Aym and Brenna

Chapter 7

Speed Limits

The Slower Partner Sets the Pace

"There is more to life than increasing its speed."

— Mahatma Gandhi

"The trees that are slow to grow bear the best fruit."

—Moliere

Chapter 7: Speed Limits

When you finally meet someone you like, and they like you, it can feel like the culmination of years of waiting and yearning. Now that you have met, you might want to charge full steam ahead into your future together. Why wait?

But let's take a moment. Does your date feel the same way? They might like you, too, but still want to take it slowly. If you start pushing and try to go too fast, you could end up losing them. Nothing is more important in a relationship than respect, and respecting your partner's desire to go at a different pace is vital.

On the other hand, maybe you're in the reverse position. Maybe you like them, but then they call you three times a day just to hear your voice and chat. Chatting on the phone may not be your idea of a good time. Why don't they text? Who calls people up to talk on the phone anymore? Tell them how you prefer to communicate and how fast or how slowly you want to go. If they don't respect your preference for style and frequency of communication in the early days, what else might they disrespect in the future? Lay out the groundwork now for what speed is okay with you and what is too fast, too much. And pay attention to their reaction to your preferences. Anyone who ignores what you want and tries to coerce you into moving forward more quickly than you're comfortable with is probably not someone you want to invest a lot of time with. You deserve to be heard and respected.

Dating While Autistic

The bottom line is the speed of progress in a relationship must always be set by the person who wants to go slowly, never by the one who wants to speed things up.

BAD IDEA/BETTER IDEA

You've had a couple of fun dates. You enjoy each other's company, laugh at the same jokes, and are in alignment on all of the major issues important to the two of you. You've moved on from a hug at the end of a date to a goodnight kiss. It seems like the right time to take this to the next level.

You have access to a friend's beach house for the weekend, and you'd love to take your date there. A weekend together sounds like a dream, and you want to make that dream come true. You invite your date for a weekend getaway, but they're not sure how they feel about that. They tell you they think it's too soon to be intimate, and a weekend holiday together sounds pretty intimate.

✗ **BAD IDEA:** You tell them it will be purely platonic, just a fun time at the beach, because that seems to be what they want to hear. You're sure that once you get there and they see the lovely house and fabulous views of the ocean, they'll change their mind and want to share a romantic, intimate weekend

Chapter 7: Speed Limits

together. You badger them into agreeing by promising separate bedrooms and a hands-off policy, and they finally, albeit somewhat reluctantly, agree.

However, you know there is only one bedroom. When you arrive, you offer them the bedroom and valiantly offer to take the lumpy couch, secretly hoping they'll take pity on you and invite you to share the bedroom with them. The more you hint about it, the more uncomfortable they appear. Now they don't even look at you; they're more engaged with their phone than with you.

Ultimately you discover that what they were doing on their phone was calling an Uber. Watching them grab their overnight bag and ride away is the last time you ever see them, because they no longer trust you.

✓ **BETTER IDEA:** When they say it's too soon for a weekend getaway together, you drop the subject. You care about this person, and you don't want to push them into making a decision they're not ready for. There will be plenty of time in your future together to plan romantic vacations, but if you come on too strong, too soon, you fear you'd scare them away.

You respect them way too much to try to convince them to go faster than they're comfortable with.

Dating While Autistic

A COUPLE OF SINGLES

Bill

After his experience at the big *Star Trek* convention, Bill was looking for something a little smaller that would still be interesting for him and that might also appeal to women in his age group with similar interests.

A local college advertised a lecture series on the history of science fiction, and the first lecture would include a showing of *Forbidden Planet*, a favorite of Bill's. Even if he didn't meet anyone there, at least he'd enjoy the movie.

After buying his ticket from a pleasant woman who seemed to be about his age but who thankfully didn't try to engage him in social chitchat, he entered the lecture hall. He went straight to the back right corner, against the wall. This was his favorite seat in any auditorium or theater. He could see and hear everything, but no one could walk behind him and trigger his peripheral "Danger, Will Robinson!" response. He hated it when people walked behind him. From his vantage point, he could see the screen perfectly, and he settled in to enjoy the movie.

He was grateful that the place was nearly empty, even though that meant less of a chance to meet someone. Not meeting someone actually felt like a relief, now that he thought about it. Better to simply enjoy the movie and lecture on his own.

Chapter 7: Speed Limits

Movement to his left alerted him to the presence of another person at the back of the hall. It was the woman who had sold him his ticket. She seemed surprised to see him but then quickly looked away and chose the seat on the back row that was farthest from him. She turned her eyes to the screen without glancing his way again, and so did he, relieved when the room darkened and the movie started.

At intermission, he noticed her at the refreshment table selling bottled water and individually packaged granola bars. He hesitated, glanced away from her before she could see him looking at her, and instead looked around the lobby. The handful of other attendees was dwindling, as many had left before the evening's lecture portion. They looked young, probably college students. He didn't get why they would watch the movie but leave before the best part. He was anxious to hear this professor's take on how the movie affected historical and modern-day science fiction. Bill suddenly felt awkward, as if he had forgotten what he was supposed to do with his arms and hands. The refreshment table now looked like a good idea. Holding a bottle of water would give him something to do.

As he approached the table, the woman looked up at him and then looked away. He ordered his water, then got a granola bar too on a whim. He could always take it home in his pocket and save it for another day. After they had exchanged money and snacks, he stood there awkwardly not knowing what to do. At this point, they were just about the only people in the lobby. He decided to say something.

"So, uh, where did everybody go? Isn't there a lecture after the movie?"

"Yes, it's the best part, but these college students don't care about anything but the movie. The only reason they even show up at all is because they're in the professor's class, and they know the movie will be on the final. They figure they can get the lectures in class and not waste their whole evening listening to him."

Bill noticed that as soon as she said this piece, she turned red and looked down at the table. Should he say something? No, he didn't want to make her more uncomfortable. Best to go back to his seat.

"Well, see you inside," he said. See you inside? He had thought it would sound cool, but as soon as the words hit the air, they sounded the opposite of cool. All at once he realized that he actually cared what this stranger thought of him, and he did not want to sound stupid. He quickly turned away from her and rushed back to his corner seat. She didn't take her seat until after the lights had gone down and the professor had tested the microphone a few times.

Throughout the lecture, Bill's attention wavered between listening to the speaker and thinking about the woman at the other end of his row. Would he speak to her afterwards before going

Chapter 7: Speed Limits

home? Would that be too much, too fast? Maybe he should wait until the second lecture in the series before he said anything else. But what if she didn't work at the other lectures? What if this was his only chance to meet her? Did she even want to meet him? Bill realized he had no idea. She might like him; she might hate him. Either way, he did not want to do anything that might push her farther away than she already was, in her own corner.

He would wait, and see what happened naturally without trying to control the outcome.

Trish

Every year Trish looked forward to her college's lecture series on the history of science fiction in film and literature. Her favorite professor was still teaching, and she loved hearing him lecture again. As an employee, she could hide behind the registration table, as she had at the reunion, and then at the refreshment table at intermission, avoiding any possibility of awkward conversations. Not that she had any interest in talking with anyone. They were mostly students, and her experience with Adam (or was it Aaron?) had put her right off trying to talk to students.

She was surprised to see a man about her age. This was unexpected. Why wasn't he out at a club or bar or a sports event, or wherever else typical men liked to gather? When he approached her to buy his ticket, she used her ticket-selling script, and he walked away. Thank goodness he didn't try to chat her up! That never went well.

As soon as everyone in the lobby had purchased their ticket and gone into the lecture hall, Trish locked up the cash box and found her own usual seat, in the back left corner, where she could keep her back to the wall. No one was going to sneak up on her!

She was startled to see the man she'd noticed earlier in the opposite corner. This was an unusual turn of events. Should she acknowledge that she remembered him from selling him his ticket? That would be stupid. Of course she remembered him; she wasn't an idiot. Usually. She sat down quickly and allowed herself to get lost in the familiar old movie.

As the end credits were rolling Trish slipped out and got set up to sell refreshments. She noticed the same guy standing around, looking a little lost. Her heart went out to him. How many times had she felt lost in a social group, until she found her solution of having a job to do? No one was buying refreshments, as most of the students left early. She was about to pack up and close when he approached her table. The interaction of purchasing and providing snacks was accomplished like clockwork. Well-rehearsed, scripted clockwork. Then he said something about the others leaving early. That got her started, and she heard herself telling him what she thought about that before she could stop herself. She bit the inside of her cheek to keep herself from going

Chapter 7: Speed Limits

on any longer than she already had and looked down, her face warm with embarrassment.

He said something about seeing her inside before he left. Had he noticed her sitting in his row? Noticing someone could be the beginning of a conversation, a friendship, a relationship. But now her thoughts were going into fast forward. Before she started naming their babies, she would focus on the present moment and not try to rush anything. No need to rush towards ultimate disappointment, like a spaceship hurtling toward a forbidden planet.

After the lecture, they both ended up in the lobby at the same time. There was an awkward silence, which Trish broke first.

"So, did you like the movie and lecture?"

"Absolutely! That movie is historical. It actually laid the groundwork for the whole *Star Trek* universe."

"I know, right? The first pilot was such an homage! The similarities are striking!"

"You know the original *Star Trek* pilot? Most people don't realize there were two of them."

"Of course. My major was historical literature, specializing in early science fiction." She noticed he looked surprised. Well, so much for that. She had shown herself to be the nerd that she was, and now she'd probably never see him again. But he wasn't making an excuse to leave. He was still there, and he was smiling. This was new.

Dating While Autistic

"Cool," he said. Then a long silence. Finally he said something else. "So, Trish, how long have you worked here at the college?"

She froze and glanced around. She was alone with a crazy stalker, and now he was between her and the exit. The college paper would carry the story of her murder, and then she would be forgotten. But not without a fight. "How do you know my name and where I work? Campus Security is already on their way here to lock up, by the way, so don't think you can try anything." She started edging around him to have a straight path to the exit.

He took two steps back away from her, his hands up, mouth open, looking distraught. Finally words came in a rush. "Your name tag! It's on your name tag!" Trish looked down. She was wearing her college employee badge with her name and where she worked. He wasn't a stalker. And she had made a fool of herself. She felt her face go hot.

"I—I am so sorry! I—" Then she began to laugh, and so did he, thankfully. Probably nervousness made them laugh longer than entirely necessary, but each time they wound down, they looked at each other and started laughing again.

Finally Bill got his breath back. "I'm Bill, by the way. It's only fair you should know my name, since I know yours. And I work at the tech company on that corner." He pointed out through the glass doors. "I mean, I used to. Now I work from home, but I go by here every day."

Chapter 7: Speed Limits

"What a small world," Trish said, smiling. Should she suggest going out for coffee? Maybe it was too soon for that. She loved having someone to laugh with, even if she was laughing at herself. It felt good, but good things could progress slowly. No need to rush.

"Will you be here for the next movie and lecture?" Bill asked.

"I'm working the whole series," she said. "I look forward to this all year."

"Then I will definitely see you again." Bill held up a hand in a Vulcan salute, which he awkwardly turned into a wave. He started walking backward toward the door, stopping himself before he tipped over a floor sign advertising the lecture series. He righted it, smiled back at her, and was gone.

Trish found herself thinking fondly of him frequently during the next week. What a lovely and unexpected turn of events! But she knew there was no need to rush things. If a friendship was meant to come of this odd first meeting, it would blossom in its own time.

ASK YOURSELF

Do you remember the story of the tortoise and the hare? Of course you do. Instead of just being a topic for cartoon take-offs, though, Aesop's original fable carried a lot of wisdom. Rushing off without true purpose and direction will not get you to the finish line or to a solid relationship. Patience and persistence will win the day. Whether you're the rabbit, reining yourself in to avoid chasing off your date, or whether you're the wise tortoise, refusing to be rushed, slow and steady is the secret to success. If you're the rabbit, ask yourself: Do you respect your date's comfort more than your desire to bring them up to your speed?

ACTUALLY AUTISTIC LOVE STORIES

At the end of our first date, I looked up at Zach and let him know (pretty bluntly) that I would like to kiss him. I asked if that would be okay. He paused at the question, and I was immediately flooded with shame, because I thought I had misread the situation. I apologized and told him to forget it.

He replied, "Well, I didn't anticipate we would kiss until the second date!"

After we kissed, he let out the sweetest giggle I had ever heard in my life. He seemed embarrassed, but I loved it. He said, "I'm not very masculine! I'm not going to be a tough guy, and I'm going to giggle and things! Is that okay?"

I looked him in the eyes and jokingly said, "I'm the boy and you're the girl," before our second kiss.

Chapter 7: Speed Limits

After we said goodbye, I lay on the couch staring at the ceiling thinking, "Oh, this is how some people say 'I love you' on the first date." My best friend texted me asking how it went with "Art Rock Cutie," and I texted back, "I'm probably going to marry him."

— Julie and Zach

Chapter 8

Happy Endings Happen

In Their Own Sweet Time

"I think we ought to live happily ever after."

— Diana Wynne Jones, *Howl's Moving Castle*

"And they lived happily (aside from a few normal disagreements, misunderstandings...and unexpected calamities) ever after."

—Jean Ferris, *Twice Upon a Marigold*

Chapter 8: Happy Endings Happen

You finally found "The One." You like them, and they seem to like you just as much. Like grew naturally to love, and now you want to spend the rest of your life with this person. That's wonderful! I'm so happy for you!

The next steps in your relationship, however, should not be rushed. If this is true love, it will withstand taking it slowly so you can both be sure. Spend time together in a variety of ways, so you can see how the two of you work together. This includes fun activities, chores, hanging out doing nothing, or going on an exciting but potentially stressful vacation together. If you've only seen one another on formal dates where everyone is on their best behavior, you don't really know each other well enough yet to plan your future.

Try washing a car together, or shopping for groceries, or cooking and cleaning up in the kitchen. IKEA is a famous relationship tester. How does your date respond to you when you get overwhelmed? How do you respond when they do? Are you both able to be patient when things don't go your way? It should never be just one person who has to compromise when you don't agree; you should feel like equally respected partners. All these things are important, and they take time.

Fortunately, you have time. Enjoy dating and hanging out and getting to know each other well. After you've spent time in many different kinds of situations, navigating difficult conversations, having arguments, negotiating conflicts and celebrating what you love about each other, you'll be in a better position to predict if this is the person you want to spend your life with.

I wish you all the best in your future. You deserve it!

BAD IDEA/BETTER IDEA

You have had several dates and find that you share a lot of interests and values. You also share some of the same sensory aversions and preferences. Whenever you're together, you have a good time. However, you don't feel as if you've been hit by Cupid's arrow, falling head over heels in love at first sight. You feel comfortable together rather than feeling swept off your feet.

✗ **BAD IDEA:** Even though you always look forward to your dates, everything you've seen on television and the movies makes you think you must be missing out if you're not totally over-the-moon lovestruck. You decide they must not really be "The One," so you call them and break up. You tell them it isn't working out between you and you want to stop dating, but you can still be friends. When they ask why, you tell them you're not attracted to them in a romantic way. They are hurt, and you feel badly for hurting them. Even though you said you wanted to still be friends, now you two avoid each other.

Chapter 8: Happy Endings Happen

Seeing them again would remind you of how you hurt them and how terrible you felt about the way it ended. You really miss spending time with them and haven't found anyone else who seems to be as compatible as you two were, but you guess that's just the way it has to be.

✓ **BETTER IDEA:** You make a list for yourself of all the things you like about this person. There are quite a few on the plus side. On the minus side, you have the lack of feeling head-over-heels in love with them. In reviewing all of the things you enjoy about them and your times together, you decide it's too soon to rule out being in love. You need to spend a lot of time doing different things. The feeling of friendship you have now could certainly grow into love, and maybe even passion. It's too soon to know for sure. In any case, their friendship is too important to risk losing it by making quick decisions. Let the future unfold for itself. Even if you never fall deeply in love with them, your friendship will continue to be precious.

A SINGULAR COUPLE

Tribble (Trish + Bill)

At the next movie and lecture in the series, Bill arrived eager to see Trish again. She was pleased to see him walk in early, and they smiled and blushed as he bought his ticket, but they didn't have much to say.

Inside, Bill started to sit in his favorite corner seat but then moved over two seats toward the center. When Trish entered their row, she paused by her corner seat and then purposefully moved over two seats closer to him. They kept their eyes on the screen during most of the movie, only occasionally glancing at each other and then quickly looking away if their eyes met.

At intermission, Trish rushed out to the refreshment table, and Bill lingered there after buying his water and granola bar. They chatted about the movie, and each of them found they felt more comfortable than they usually did in social conversations. He waited while she locked up the cash box, and when they returned for the lecture, they naturally sat together in the center of the back row. This became their habit for the next couple of lectures, until they each confessed they felt more comfortable in an actual corner than they did in the center. After that, they took turns sitting in their preferred corner with the other one beside them as a cushion against the rest of the world. Switching corners each time let each

Chapter 8: Happy Endings Happen

of them experience feeling protected and the protector in some small way. It felt good.

After the second lecture, they chatted for a long time in the parking lot. After the third lecture, it started to rain while they were still talking, so they went to a nearby coffee shop. There was a moment of awkwardness when the check came.

Bill had his hand on the check before he thought, was he being sexist by picking it up because he was the man? Was that presumptuous? Was this a date or just a meeting between two friends? Now that he had his hand on the check but hadn't moved to actually pay it, would she think he didn't want to pay it after all? Would he look cheap? How long had he been sitting here with his hand on the check not doing anything?

Trish wondered if she should offer to split the check, but that felt petty. Anyway, she couldn't do even simple math when she was stressed. Dating was stressful even if it was fun. Wait, dating? Was that what they were doing? If he thought it was a date, and then she offered to split it, would he think she didn't want it to be a date? And why should the man always pay for dates, anyway? What was this, the twentieth century?

They were both frozen for several moments staring at the check in Bill's hand. Finally Trish picked up her purse. Spurred back into action by the movement, Bill picked up the check.

"Let me get this," he said.

Dating While Autistic

Trish put her purse back down and said, "Only if you let me get the next one."

Bill smiled. "The next one?"

"Yes, we could take turns treating each other. Everyone likes to be treated sometimes, right?"

"Right, yes, right, let's take turns." Bill couldn't stop smiling. "Of course you realize, we will have to go out an even number of times if we want it to be fair."

Trish nodded. "Agreed. Thank you for the coffee, and I look forward to our next meeting." They were both smiling now.

From then on, they always went to the same coffee shop after each lecture, and they talked for hours. He told her everything he loved about the original *Star Trek* series, and she shared about the history of science fiction in literature and film that she had studied.

After the lecture series was over, they found a TED Talk "Best Of" series in the college library, and they started attending that together. It was a much smaller venue, but they always found a corner in the back where they could sit together and feel comfortable. It was always exciting to go out afterward and discuss what they had heard. One of the TED Talks was by Dr. Temple Grandin, and Bill decided to come out of the autism closet and tell Trish that he was autistic, like Dr. Grandin. Trish started laughing so hard that he regretted opening up to her. Why had he told her he was autistic?

Chapter 8: Happy Endings Happen

What would she think of him now? As she tried to control her laughter, she kept pointing to herself. Finally she got out the words, "Me, too!"

"You're autistic, too? You're not just saying that?"

"Of course I'm autistic. I didn't realize you were. I thought we just had a lot in common."

"We do have a lot in common."

"I guess now we have one more thing." They each reached at the same time and realized they were holding hands for the first time. Now it was definitely a date.

That night as they stood by their cars in the lot, Bill asked Trish out for dinner. He made it clear that he was talking about a date, and she happily accepted. They continued their tradition of taking turns treating, so the next time, Trish asked Bill out for dinner. Each time they met for a meal, they chose the restaurant in advance so they could look up the menu online. It was so much less stressful when they had pre-planned their meal and didn't have to think about it.

After their second dinner date, lingering in the parking lot, Bill said, "I'm thinking about a hug. Would you want a hug goodnight?"

"Yes, I'd like a hug, thank you. What about a kiss, too?"

Their first hug and kiss were a bit awkward, as are everyone's firsts, but it marked the beginning of what would be a long and loving relationship.

Dating While Autistic

For Bill and Trish, taking their time and not trying to rush romance was exactly right for them.

ASK YOURSELF

Have you found the date of your dreams yet? If you have, congratulations! Enjoy getting to know each other. If you haven't, though, remember that these things take time. Have you given up? No? Are you still open to opportunities? The future is filled to the brim with possibility. Enjoy your continuing adventure!

ACTUALLY AUTISTIC LOVE STORIES

I had a crush on Wendy, a woman in my writers' support group, for a long time. My friend, Greg, knew it, and he kept pushing me to ask her out. For a long time I couldn't bring myself to do it, but then an event came up where I could bring a "plus one." Greg made me promise to ask her and I agreed, even though I was sure she'd turn me down. I put it off as long as I could, until almost the last minute. I almost hoped it would be too late for her to make it, because then at least I could tell Greg I tried.

Chapter 8: Happy Endings Happen

When Wendy picked up the phone, I was nervous, but I put on a confident persona and came right to the point. It turned out she liked me, too. I had no idea! We went on the date, and (long story short) we fell in love. We were married within a year of our first date. I can't imagine what my life would have been like if I hadn't made that phone call.

— A memory previously told by David, late-diagnosed autistic man

After our first date and that first kiss that made Zach giggle, I broke it off with every other suitor immediately and never looked back. I forced myself to take other steps more slowly, but it turns out I was right from the first night.

A little over three years later, we were married.

— Julie and Zach

We never did things the traditional way. Shortly after our big talk, when I finally went for it and told him exactly how I felt and he not only felt the same way but loved me, we got engaged. We've been together for nearly five years now. Throughout our relationship, he has learned to embrace my full self, as I embrace him.

— Ana, autism/ADHD, married to NT man

Dating While Autistic

We said "I love you" after only a week, got engaged after eight months, and married another nine months after that. August 2022 was our fourth wedding anniversary.

Over the years, we have supported each other and helped each other grow. We learned so much about ourselves just by being able to fully unmask and live in a safe and supportive environment. We have a small and quiet life that works perfectly for our needs and feel very lucky to have found each other.

— Aym and Brenna

My favorite thing about being married to Elliot is our ability to tell things like they are. We communicate with each other honestly and express ourselves as best we can. Our first date was nine years ago, and our marriage is stronger than ever.

— Marian

Eleven years after that surprise proposal when I thought he was breaking up with me, and one autism diagnosis later, we realize how well our neurodivergences complement one another. My autistic need for structure and organization helps keep his ADHD self on task and able to find his keys. His spontaneous ADHD brain helps me safely release control and be less rigid, even if it's

Chapter 8: Happy Endings Happen

letting him treat me to takeaway on a night I had already planned to cook.

That's my "happily ever after." I've learned to make space for spontaneous acts of care and love. I know now that my world doesn't collapse just because something unexpected happened.

After all, there is nothing planned or controlled about love!

— Tara, autistic woman married to a man with ADHD

Acknowledgments

So many people have helped bring this book from idea to page.
I am incredibly fortunate to have been...

- guided by Rose Heredia-Bechtel, Susan Thompson, Jennifer Gilpin Yacio, and the entire team at Future Horizons, Inc. I appreciate you all so much!
- taught by first readers and editors Cynthia Whitcomb and Siobhan Marsh, and sensitivity reader Cat Marsh, who helped make this book better than I thought it would be.
- encouraged by writers and friends, Cherie Walters, Cynthia Whitcomb, Diane Hagood, Kristi Negri, Laura Whitcomb, Linda Leslie, Pamela Smith Hill, and Susan Fletcher.
- uplifted by my children, Cat, Siobhan, and Noel; my siblings, Jonathan, Cynthia, and Laura; and the memory of my parents, David and Susanne, and my true love David.
- inspired and moved by the people who shared their own autism love stories for this book: Ana, Aym, Doug, Julie, Kelsey, Marian, and Tara. Thank you for sharing your authenticity and your lived experiences! Your stories have enriched and added heart to this little book!

Thank you all!

This is part of an ongoing series called
Adulting While Autistic.

It explores the facets of a neuromajority adulthood, including dating, marriage, parenthood and more.

Wendela Whitcomb Marsh explores the many ways autists can succeed and be true to themselves in a neuromajority world.

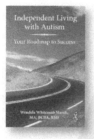

Independent Living with Autism

Dating While Autistic

Relating While Autistic *(Coming June 2023)*

Parenting While Autistic *(Coming in 2024)*

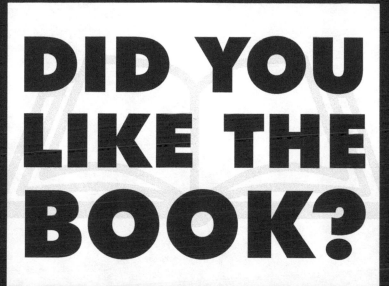

DID YOU LIKE THE BOOK?

Rate it and share your opinion.

amazon.com

BARNES&NOBLE
BOOKSELLERS
www.bn.com

Not what you expected? Tell us!

Most negative reviews occur when the book did not reach expectation. Did the description build any expectations that were not met? Let us know how we can do better.

Please drop us a line at *info@fhautism.com*.

Thank you so much for your support!

FUTURE HORIZONS

CPSIA information can be obtained
at www.ICGtesting.com
Printed in the USA
JSHW030019131222
34704JS00001B/1

9 781949 177992